PIANO MUSIC
BY BRITISH AND AMERICAN COMPOSERS

INTERMEDIATE TO EARLY ADVANCED LEVEL

26 Works by 17 Composers

ISBN 978-1-4950-6228-5

BOOSEY&HAWKES

AN IMAGEM COMPANY

DISTRIBUTED BY

HAL•LEONARD®
CORPORATION

7777 W. BLUEMOUND RD. P.O. BOX 13819 MILWAUKEE, WI 53213

www.boosey.com
www.halleonard.com

CONTENTS

COMPOSER BIOGRAPHIES

ARTHUR BENJAMIN
(1893–1960)

Arthur Benjamin was born in Sydney, Australia, and received his earliest education in Brisbane. Even as a boy, he was determined to pursue his musical training in London, and in 1911 he achieved his aim, studying composition with Sir Charles Villiers Stanford and piano with Frederick Cliffe. At the outbreak of war in 1914 Benjamin joined the army, later transferring to the RAF. His plane was shot down and he was captured. After the war he returned to Australia, but he soon found the atmosphere too restrictive, and in 1921 returned to England. In 1926 he took up a professorship of piano at the Royal College of Music, where his students included the young Benjamin Britten. Benjamin wrote several operas, a symphony, and a *Romantic Fantasy* for violin, viola and orchestra (premiered by Jascha Heifetz and William Primrose in 1938), among other works. He wrote music for films, including Hitchcock's *The Man Who Knew Too Much*, for which he composed an extended *Storm Clouds Cantata*. In addition to his composing activities, Benjamin was a conductor of note; he was music director of the Vancouver Symphony Orchestra for five years (1941–46). The *Jamaican Rumba*, published in 1938, brought Benjamin popular acclaim, making him something of a household name, so much so that the Jamaican government assigned him a free barrel of rum a year for his contribution to making the country known.

LEONARD BERNSTEIN
(1918–1990)

Born in Lawrence, Massachusetts, Bernstein was a groundbreaking presence in twentieth century American music, with compositions that ranged from Broadway musicals to progressive concert works. After piano studies in his youth, he was educated at Harvard and the Curtis Institute of Music. His career as a conductor began with a splash in 1943 when he substituted for an ill Bruno Walter in a nationally broadcast New York Philharmonic concert. He was the first American to rise to international prominence as a conductor, appearing for decades with all the world's major orchestras in a large repertoire. From 1958 until 1969 he was musical director of the New York Philharmonic. Bernstein was

a multi-media presence, making hundreds of recordings and appearing often on television, especially in his lecture series "Omnibus." Politically active throughout his life, a 1989 performance he conducted of Beethoven's Symphony No. 9 celebrating the fall of the Berlin Wall was viewed by 100 million people around the world. Bernstein was a skilled pianist, and early in his career he often performed in that capacity with orchestras, usually conducting a concerto from the piano. He composed regularly from his teens until his death, and wrote symphonies and other orchestral works, piano music, chamber music, song cycles and vocal works, and choral pieces, such as his often performed *Chichester Psalms*. Bernstein composed three ballets, two operas, film scores, and the Broadway musicals *On the Town*, *Wonderful Town*, *Candide* and *West Side Story*. *Four Anniversaries*, like Virgil Thomson's *Portraits* (also in this book), is a collection of short musical tributes for people Bernstein knew personally: Felicia Montealegre, his future wife, Johnny Mehegan, a New York-based jazz pianist, David Diamond, a fellow composer, and Helen Coates, Bernstein's childhood piano teacher and later his personal secretary.

FRANK BRIDGE
(1879–1941)

Frank Bridge enjoyed a varied musical career as a composer, chamber musician, and conductor. He studied violin and composition at the Royal College of Music beginning in 1899, and played in the English String Quartet for several years following graduation. He gained a reputation as a reliable conductor to substitute on short notice, even for such high-profile events as the Promenade Concerts. He was also noted as Benjamin Britten's composition teacher. Over time, Bridge's compositional work evolved from a late-romantic style to one that embraced dissonance and non-triadic interval structures. His substantial body of chamber music includes four string quartets, two piano trios, a cello sonata, and a violin sonata. His piano sonata is one of the most significant British contributions to the genre. He also wrote orchestral music, including *The Sea*. In 1923 Bridge traveled to the United States to conduct his own music in New York, Boston, Cleveland, and Detroit. The pieces contained in *Three Sketches* date back to the first years of Bridge's professional career.

BENJAMIN BRITTEN
(1913–1976)

Britten was the most often performed and recorded British composer of the twentieth century, and his music has become a central part of the international repertoire. Born in Suffolk, he began composition as a child. He studied with Frank Bridge, and at the Royal College of Music in London, studying with Arthur Benjamin, Harold Samuel and John Ireland. A dedicated pacifist, he left for the U.S. in 1939, returning to the U.K. in 1942. As a pianist he accompanied tenor Peter Pears, his life partner, for decades in recital and on recordings, and conducted performances and many recordings of his own works. Britten achieved public recognition early on, with regular BBC broadcasts. His international fame grew quickly after the vast success of the opera *Peter Grimes*, premiered in 1945. Britten was a prolific composer, working in many genres. He composed 16 operas, most of which are regularly produced, orchestral works, and chamber music. He created a substantial body of beloved choral music, the masterwork *War Requiem* among them. Britten also wrote a large number of vocal works, including song cycles, folksong arrangements, and pieces for voice and orchestra. He wrote dozens of realizations of music by Henry Purcell. Britten's importance to British cultural life was enhanced by his founding of the English Opera Group in 1946 and the Aldeburgh Festival two years later. Britten never fully recovered from heart surgery in 1973, and died at age 63 a few months after being appointed a life peer and given the title of Baron, the first composer ever granted that honor. Though a pianist himself, Britten wrote relatively few pieces for solo piano. He was 20 when he composed *Holiday Diary* in October of 1934. It was titled *New Studies* at its first performance, then was published in 1935 as *Holiday Tales*. Britten later changed the title. The set was dedicated to his teacher, Arthur Benjamin. *Night-Piece (Notturno)* was completed in 1963 for the Leeds International Piano Competition.

ELLIOT CARTER
(1908–2012)

Elliott Carter is internationally respected as one America's leading voices of the classical music tradition. He was one of the few living composers to be inducted into the American Classical Music Hall of Fame during his lifetime, and was recognized by the Pulitzer Prize Committee for the first time in 1960 for his groundbreaking *String Quartet No. 2*. Igor Stravinsky hailed Carter's *Double Concerto* for harpsichord, piano, and two chamber orchestras (1961) and *Piano Concerto* (1967), as "masterpieces." Carter's prolific career spanned over 75 years, with more than 150 pieces, ranging from chamber music to orchestra to opera, often marked with a sense of wit and humor. His astonishing late-career creative burst resulted in a number of brief solo and chamber works. Carter showed his mastery in larger forms as well, with major contributions such as *What Next?* (1997–98), *Three Illusions for Orchestra* (2004), and a piano concerto, *Interventions* (2007), which premiered on Carter's 100th birthday concert at Carnegie Hall with James Levine, Daniel Barenboim, and the Boston Symphony Orchestra (December 11, 2008). His other works for piano include the early *Piano Sonata* (1945-46) and *Night Fantasies* (1980). Elliott Carter's note on 90+: "90+ for piano is built around ninety short, accented notes played in a slow regular beat. Against these the context changes character continually. It was composed in March of 1994 to celebrate the ninetieth birthday of my dear and much admired friend, Goffredo Petrassi, Italy's leading composer of his generation."

AARON COPLAND
(1900–1990)

Aaron Copland's name is synonymous with American music. In addition to writing such well-loved works as *Fanfare for the Common Man*, *Rodeo*, and the Pulitzer Prize-winning *Appalachian Spring*, Copland conducted, organized concerts, wrote books on music, and served as an American cultural ambassador to the world. While studying with Nadia Boulanger in Paris, Copland became interested in incorporating popular styles into his music. Upon his return to the U.S. he advanced the cause of new music through lectures and writings, and organized the famed Copland-Sessions concerts. Throughout his career, he nurtured the careers of others, including Leonard Bernstein, Carlos Chavez, Toru Takemitsu, and David Del Tredici. He took up conducting while in his fifties, becoming a persuasive interpreter of his own music; he continued to conduct in concerts, on the radio, and on television until he was 83. In 1982, The Aaron Copland School of Music was established in his honor at Queens College of the City University of New York. *The Cat and the Mouse*, one of Copland's first published works, is based on the fable of The Old Cat and the Young Mouse by Jean de la Fontaine. Copland left *Midday Thoughts* unfinished in the 1940s but returned to it decades later when an assistant rediscovered the piece. The composer described it as "a brief lyric piece very much in the manner of *Appalachian Spring*." *The Passacaglia* dates back to his study with Nadia Boulanger in Paris, where he was trained in the mastery of traditional forms.

PETER MAXWELL DAVIES
(b. 1934)

Peter Maxwell Davies rose to prominence in late 1960s with neo-expressionistic music-theatre pieces *Eight Songs for a Mad King*, *Vesalii Icones*, and *Miss Donnithorne's Maggot*. His major theatrical works include the operas *Taverner*, *The Martyrdom of St Magnus* and *The Doctor of Myddfai*, and the full-length ballet *Salome*. His large output of orchestral works includes eight symphonies and thirteen concertos, as well as the highly popular *An Orkney Wedding with Sunrise*. Davies's output for solo piano consists of a sonata, several short suites, and early student pieces. Davies was Associate Conductor/Composer of the BBC Philharmonic and Royal Philharmonic Orchestras for a ten-year period, and then became Composer Laureate of the Scottish Chamber Orchestra, for whom he has written a series of ten *Strathclyde Concertos*. In 1987 Davies was knighted and in 2004 he was appointed Master of the Queen's Music. He lives in the Orkney Islands off the north coast of Scotland, where he writes most of his music. *Farewell to Stromness* and *Yesnaby Ground* are interludes from *The Yellow Cake Revue*. Davies wrote this suite in 1980 in response to a Scottish government report about the possibility of mining uranium on the Orkney Islands. The tiny movements of *Five Little Pieces* employ serial techniques, and *Three Sanday Places* is a set of miniatures in which Davies explores the special character of his island home of Sanday.

DAVID DEL TREDICI
(b. 1937)

Generally recognized as the father of the Neo-Romantic movement in music, David Del Tredici has received numerous awards and has been commissioned and performed by nearly every major American and European orchestral ensemble. He was awarded the Pulitzer Prize in 1980 for *In Memory of a Summer Day* for soprano and orchestra. Much of his early work consisted of elaborate vocal settings of James Joyce and Lewis Carroll. His major works include the orchestral song cycles *Final Alice* (1975) and *Child Alice* (1981). More recently, Del Tredici has set to music a cavalcade of contemporary American poets, often celebrating a gay sensibility. He was a longtime Distinguished Professor of Music at The City College of New York. He makes his home in Greenwich Village. *Aeolian Ballade* is, in the composer's own words, "an elaborately developed prelude and fugue". In the middle of the fugue, a dolce section emerges, built on the letters/notes G-R(re)-A-C-E. This is a reference to Grace Cloutier, who commissioned the original version of the piece for harp.

FREDERICK DELIUS
(1862–1934)

Frederick Delius was born on 29 January 1862 in Bradford, Yorkshire, the son of German-born parents who had emigrated to England to participate in the wool-trade, then one of Britain's most successful export industries. He enrolled as a student at the New York Conservatorium from 1886-88, before returning to Europe and settling in Paris, where he stayed for ten years. Delius composed operas including *Koanga* and *A Village Romeo and Juliet*, orchestral works such as *Brigg Fair: An English Rhapsody*, a piano concerto, and the ambitious *Mass of Life* for chorus and orchestra. Although Edvard Grieg was an early friend and supporter (and influence), Delius's social circle was more often populated with painters rather than musicians, and his friends included Edvard Munch and Paul Gauguin. He also married a painter, the German-born Helena ('Jelka') Rosen. Sometime between 1896 and 1900 Delius contracted syphilis and during the First World War his health began to fail. He began to lose the use of his limbs, and his eyesight grew steadily worse. By 1920 he was unable to compose. A young English musician by the name of Eric Fenby offered his services as amanuensis, and with his help Delius produced several more works before his death. *Five Piano Pieces*, composed in 1923, features a melody to be either hummed by the pianist or played on a violin in No. 4.

CARLISLE FLOYD
(b. 1926)

Carlisle Floyd is one of the foremost American composers and librettists of opera. He earned B.M. and M.M. degrees in piano and composition at Syracuse University, taught at Florida State University from 1947-1976, and then accepted the prestigious M. D. Anderson Professorship in the University of Houston. In addition, he was co-founder with David Gockley of the Houston Opera Studio jointly created by the University of Houston and Houston Grand Opera. He first achieved national prominence with his opera *Susannah* (1953–54), performed by the New York City Opera in 1956 after its world premiere at Florida State University in 1955. *Of Mice and Men* (1969) is Floyd's other most often performed work. Based on the Steinbeck novel, it was commissioned by the Ford Foundation and was given its premiere by the Seattle Opera in 1970. Floyd's more recent operas, *Bilby's Doll* (1976), *Willie Stark* (1981), and *Cold Sassy Tree* (2000) were produced by the Houston Grand Opera. Non-operatic works include an orchestral song cycle, *Citizen of Paradise* (1984), and a large-scale work for chorus, bass-baritone soloist, and orchestra titled *A Time to Dance* (1993), commissioned by the American Choral Directors Association.

JOHN IRELAND
(1879–1962)

John Ireland was born in Bowden, Cheshire, into a highly cultured environment (though his parents' interests were literary rather than musical). He studied piano at the Royal College of Music in London from 1893 to 1897, continuing at the College until 1901 as a composition scholar, under Sir Charles Villiers Stanford. His fellow students at the RCM included Vaughan Williams and Holst. He earned his Ph.D. from Durham University in 1906, and was later (1932) to be awarded an honorary doctorate there. From 1904 until 1926 Ireland held the post of organist at St Luke's, Chelsea, which allowed him time to compose. He also gained a strong reputation as a much-respected teacher at the Royal College of Music as Professor of Composition; his pupils there included Benjamin Britten. Ireland had been composing since boyhood but, fiercely self-critical, he destroyed all his early works; the earliest surviving work in his catalogue therefore dates only from 1903. His Second Violin Sonata made such an impact on its first performance that the first edition was sold out even before it was published. His song *Sea Fever* (1913), to a text by Masefield, is still one of the best-known British art-songs. His church music swiftly entered the repertoire and was sung throughout Britain. And for many years his *Piano Concerto* (1930) was a favourite at the Proms.

KARL JENKINS
(b. 1944)

Karl Jenkins is one of the most performed living composers in the world. He was born in Wales and educated at Gowerton Grammar School before studying music at the University of Wales, Cardiff. He then commenced postgraduate studies at the Royal Academy of Music, London. Karl holds a Doctor of Music degree from the University of Wales, and has been made both a Fellow and an Associate of the Royal Academy of Music, where a room has been named in his honour. Jenkins's *Adiemus project*, combining classical with ethnic vocal sounds and percussion with an invented language, topped classical and pop charts around the world. *The Armed Man: A Mass for Peace* has been performed over 1800 times in

20 different countries since the CD was released. His other output includes the harp concerto *Over the Stone* commissioned by HRH the Prince of Wales for the Royal Harpist, Catrin Finch, *Euphonium Concerto* for David Childs, and the concertante *Quirk*, commissioned by the London Symphony Orchestra and conducted by Sir Colin Davies as part of its 2005 centenary season. As a conductor Karl has appeared on the rostrum in the Royal Albert Hall and Royal Festival Hall in London, the Welsh Millennium Centre and St David's Hall in Cardiff, and Carnegie Hall and Lincoln Center in New York, as well as conducting performances of his music as far afield as Johannesburg, Mumbai, Hong Kong, Beijing and Tokyo. *Madog* is a showpiece with boogie-woogie inflections.

BENJAMIN LEES
(1924–2010)

Benjamin Lees spent his early years in San Francisco, moving to Los Angeles with his family in 1939. Following military service in WWII he attended the University of Southern California. Later he began four years of intensive private study with the composer George Antheil. He taught at the Peabody Conservatory, the Juilliard School, the Manhattan School of Music, and Queens College, New York. His works have been performed by major orchestras such as the New York Philharmonic and Royal Philharmonic Orchestra, London. Major soloists performing his music have included pianists Ian Hobson, Emanuel Ax, and Gary Graffman, and the Tokyo String Quartet. Lees received two Guggenheim Fellowships, was the first recipient of the Fromm Foundation Award in 1952, and was invited as a guest of the Union of Soviet Composers in 1967. The composer's major orchestral works include five symphonies, four concertos, and *Passacaglia for Orchestra*. *Piano Sonata No. 4*, *Mirrors*, and *Fantasy Variations* are notable works for piano. The *Toccata*, composed in 1953, is full of technical challenges, from huge leaps in both hands to sequences of fast octaves.

MEREDITH MONK
(b. 1942)

Meredith Monk is a composer, singer, and creator of new opera and music theater works, and a pioneer in what is now called "extended vocal technique" and "interdisciplinary performance". She holds honorary Doctor of Arts degrees from Bard College, the University of the Arts, The Juilliard School, the San Francisco Art Institute and the Boston Conservatory. In 1965 Monk began her innovative exploration of the voice as a multi-faceted instrument and subsequently composed and performed many solo pieces for unaccompanied voice and voice/keyboard. In 1978 she formed Meredith Monk & Vocal Ensemble to further expand her musical textures and forms. Her music has been performed by numerous soloists and groups including The Chorus of the San Francisco Symphony, Kitka, Musica Sacra, The Pacific Mozart Ensemble, Double Edge, and Bang on a Can All-Stars, among others. In October 1999 Monk performed a *Vocal Offering* for His Holiness, the Dalai Lama, as part of the World Festival of Sacred Music in Los Angeles. *Railroad (Travel Song)* was composed in 1981 for the opera *Specimen Days*. It was inspired by *Notes of a Pianist*, the travel diary of composer Louis Moreau Gottschalk, which describes his journeys and concerts during the Civil War. Monk writes about *Window in 7's*: "…even though the right and the left hands are dealing with two different sound worlds, allowing them to relate will help bring about a more expressive overall sound."

NED ROREM
(b. 1923)

Winner of the Pulitzer Prize and a Grammy, Rorem has composed three symphonies, four piano concertos, and an array of other orchestral works; music for numerous combinations of chamber forces; ten operas; choral works of every description; ballets and other music for the theater; and hundreds of art songs. He is the author of sixteen books, including five volumes of diaries and collections of lectures and criticism. At age seventeen, Rorem entered the Music School of Northwestern University, and two years later receiving a scholarship to the Curtis Institute in Philadelphia. He studied composition under Bernard Wagenaar at Juilliard, where he earned both his Bachelor's and Master's degrees. In January 2000 Rorem was elected President of the American Academy of Arts and Letters. His suite *Air Music* won the 1976 Pulitzer Prize in music. The Atlanta Symphony recording of the *String Symphony*, *Sunday Morning*, and *Eagles* received a Grammy Award for Outstanding Orchestral Recording in 1989. In 1998 he was chosen Composer of the Year by Musical America. Rorem's operas include *Miss Julie*, *Three Sisters Who Are Not Sisters*, and *Our Town*, a setting of the Thornton Wilder play. The miniatures contained in *Six Friends* are tributes to actress Marian Seldes, Ned's sister Rosemary, pianist Jerome Lowenthal, and others.

ALEC ROWLEY
(1892–1958)

Pianist and composer Alec Rowley studied at the Royal Academy of Music. In 1920 he joined the staff of Trinity College of Music, and in 1934 he became a fellow of the Royal Academy of Music. He also held the position of organist at St. Alban's Church in Teddington for many years. His compositional output includes many pieces for piano, some of which are for educational purposes, two piano concertos, and *The Sailor's Garland*, a seven-part song cycle for mixed choir. *Old English Worthies* is a collection of short pieces by eighteenth-century English composers, originally written for lute or organ. Rowley adapted and edited the music for piano, publishing the complete volume in 1917.

VIRGIL THOMSON
(1896–1989)

Virgil Thomson grew up studying both piano and organ, eventually working as an organist at a church in his hometown of Kansas City. During World War I he enlisted in the army and trained in aviation. In 1919 he enrolled at Harvard, where he studied orchestration and contemporary French music with the French-trained composer Edward Burlingame Hill. He also held the position of accompanist and assistant to the Harvard Glee Club for three years. After graduation, Thomson lived in Paris until 1940. He studied organ and counterpoint with Nadia Boulanger, and also met the poet Gertrude Stein, collaborating with her on an opera, *Four Saints in Three Acts*. After the opera, Thomson focused on instrumental works, producing two string quartets, a violin sonata, and more. Upon returning to the United States, he became chief music critic of the *New York Herald Tribune*, continued to compose, and won a Pulitzer Prize for his film score *Louisiana Story* in 1948. Later operas included *The Mother of us all* (with another libretto by Gertrude Stein) and *Lord Byron*. Thomson's musical style was diverse, combining elements of nineteenth-century popular songs and hymns, Gregorian chant, and some influence from Satie, whom he met in France. The selections from *Portraits* are short tributes to Thomson's friends, including painter Franco Assetto, soprano Marya Freund, and fellow composer Aaron Copland.

Jamaican Rumba

Arranged for Piano Solo by
ARTHUR BENJAMIN
(1938)

Four Anniversaries

1. For Felicia Montealegre
(Feb. 6, 1922)

LEONARD BERNSTEIN
(1948)

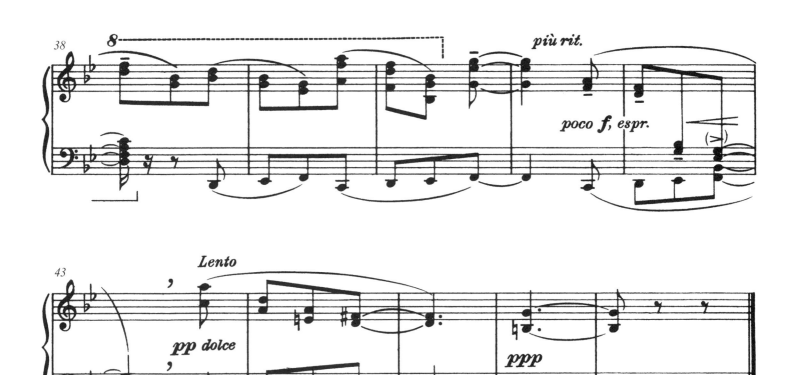

2. For Johnny Mehegan
(June 6, 1920)

3. For David Diamond
(July 9, 1915)

Poco più mosso

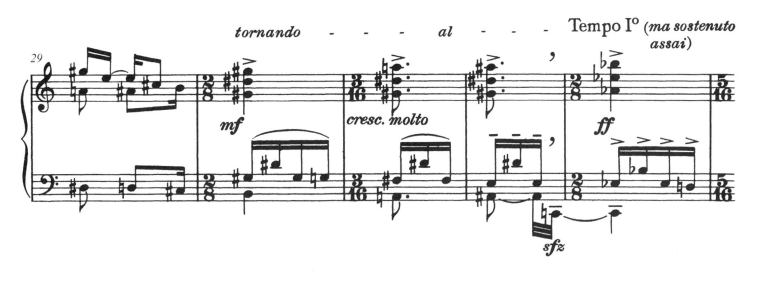

4. For Helen Coates
(July 19, 1899)

Three Sketches
April

FRANK BRIDGE
(1906)

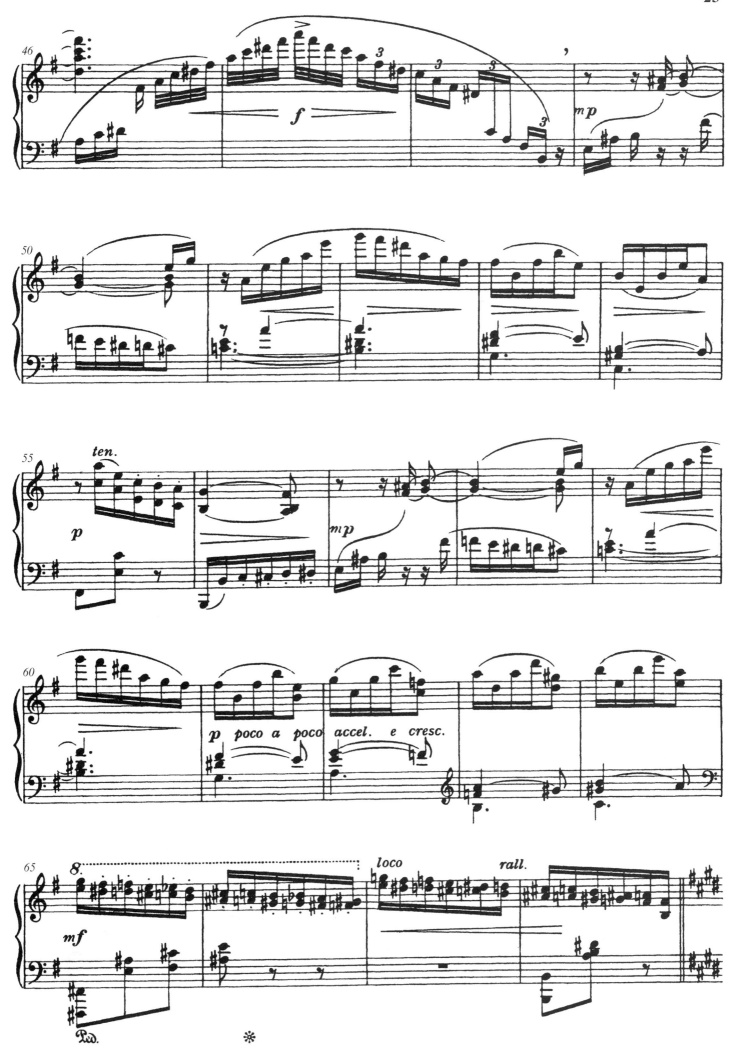

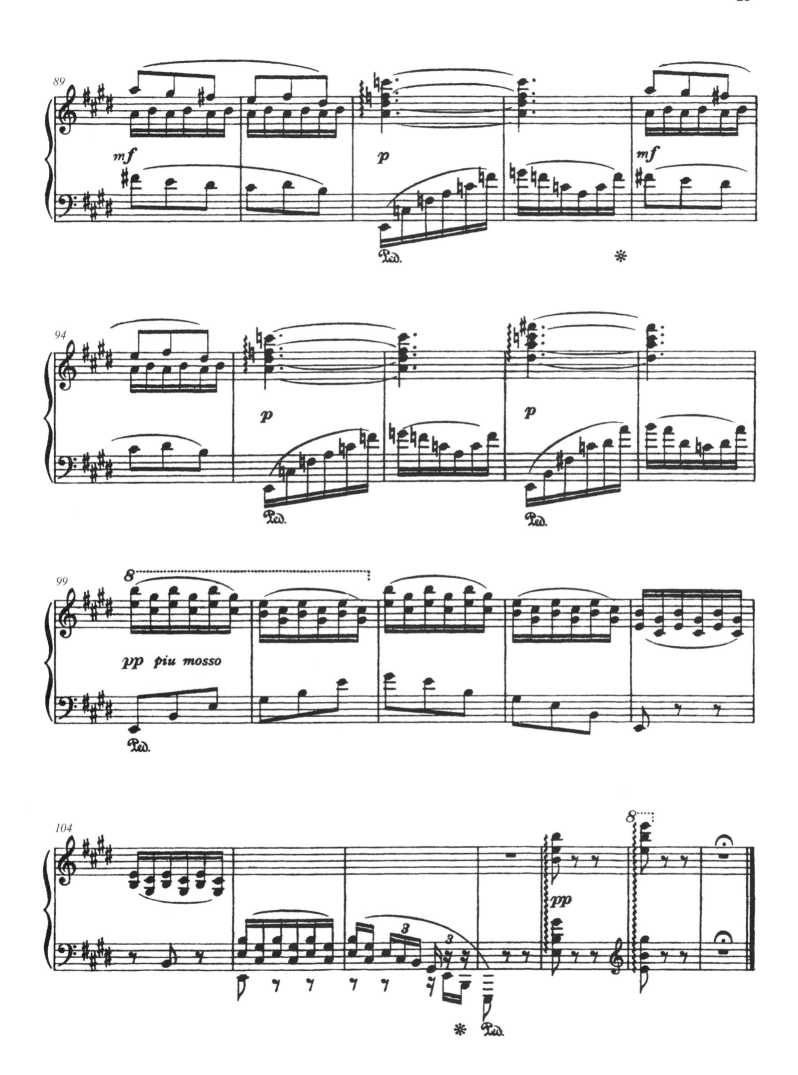

Rosemary

Valse Capricieuse

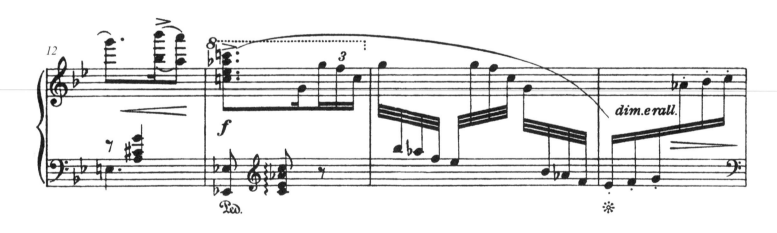

Night-Piece
(Notturno)

BENJAMIN BRITTEN
(1963)

*These notes should be silently pressed
down before the pedal is released.

To Arthur Benjamin

Holiday Diary
1. Early Morning Bathe

BENJAMIN BRITTEN
Op. 5
(1934)

WINTHROP ROGERS EDITION

Oct. 3rd 1934

2. Sailing

Molto animando

Oct. 9th 1934

3. Fun-fair

⊕ Half-pedal each quaver

Oct. 12th 1934

4. Night

Oct. 11th 1934

mille e novanta auguri a caro Goffredo

90+

ELLIOTT CARTER
(1994)

(senza pedale)*

* Use pedal only to join one chord to another *legato,* as in mm. 1–13, 16–21, 36–43, and 45–48.

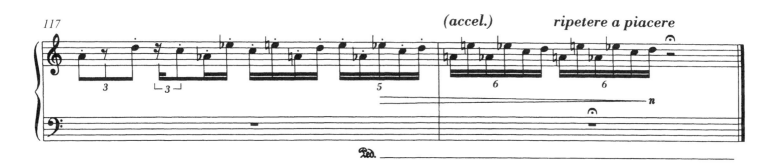

To Bennett Lerner

Midday Thoughts

AARON COPLAND
(1982)

Tempo II, calmato

* Grace-note for small hands only.

** Don't lose top voice.

The Cat and the Mouse
Scherzo Humoristique

AARON COPLAND
(1920)

To Mlle. Nadia Boulanger

Passacaglia

AARON COPLAND
(1922)

Quasi doppio movimento ($\textit{♩}$= 84)

Farewell to Stromness

from *The Yellow Cake Revue*

PETER MAXWELL DAVIES
(1980)

Five Little Pieces
1.

PETER MAXWELL DAVIES
(1960-64)

Cirenchester 1960

2.

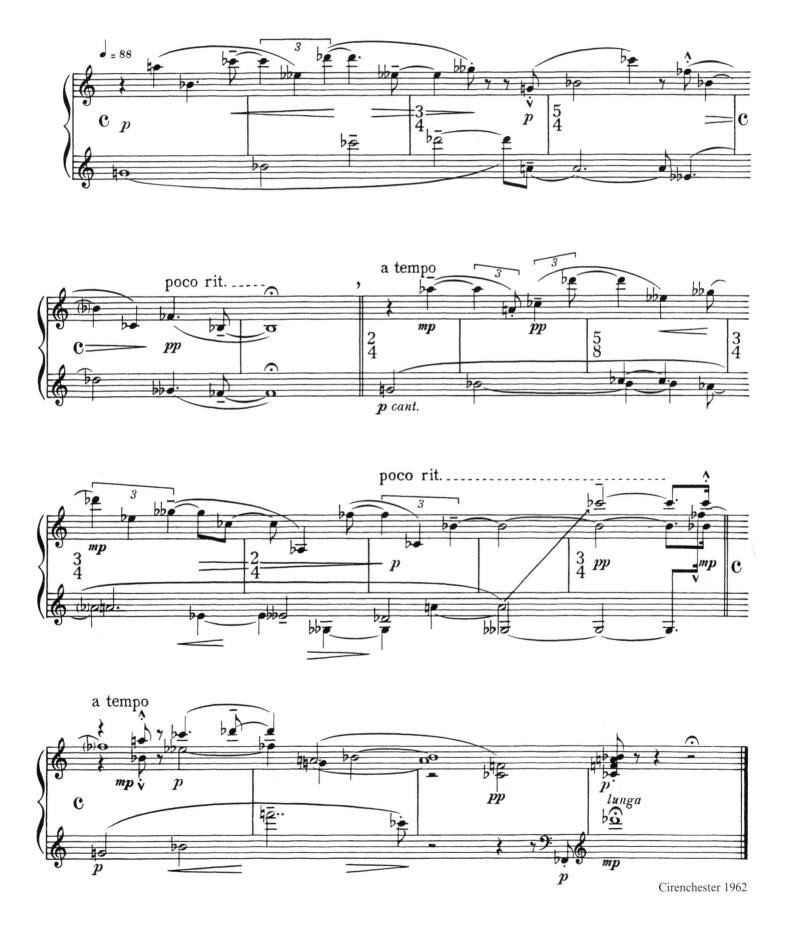

Cirenchester 1962

3.

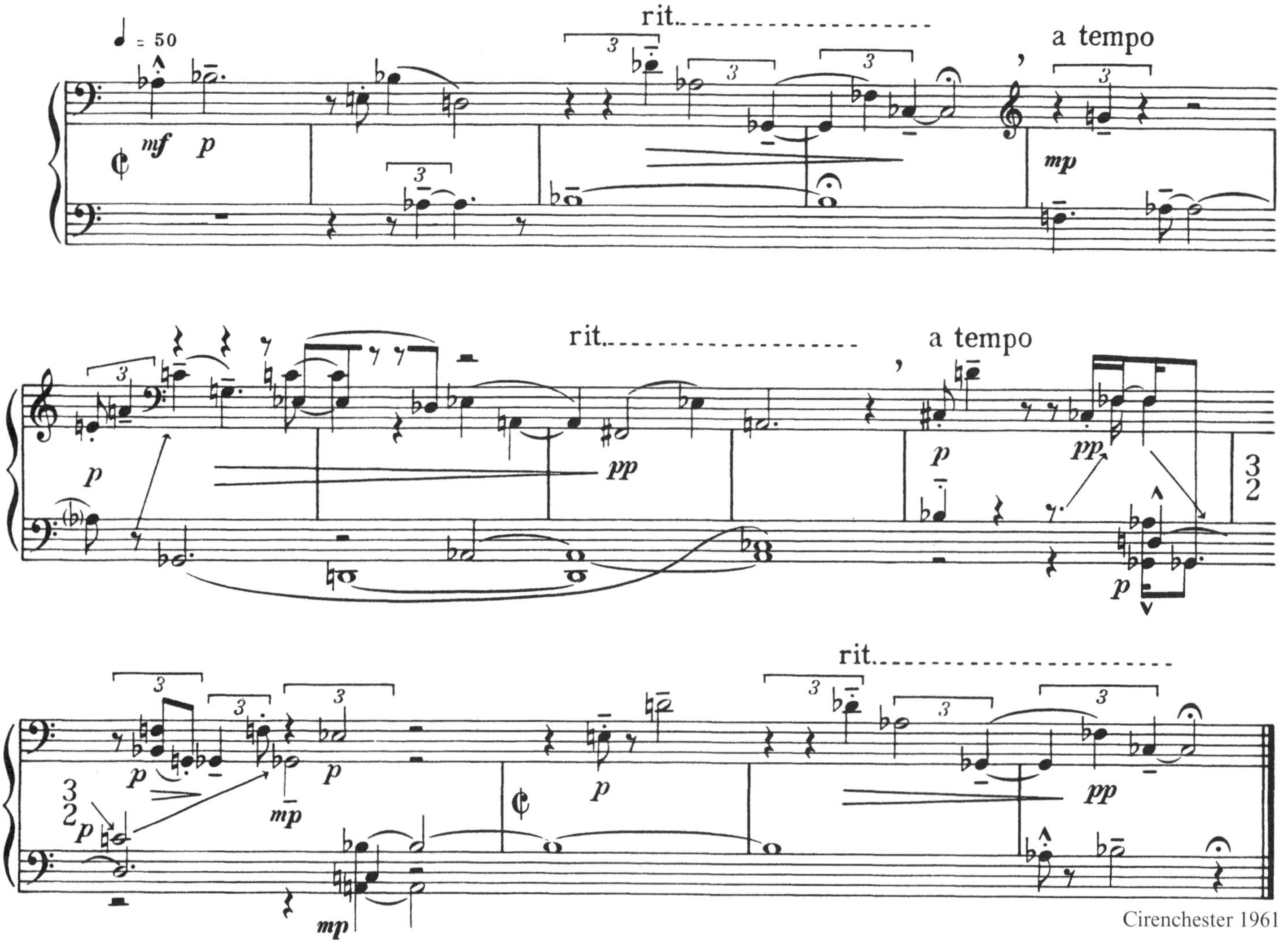

Cirenchester 1961

4.

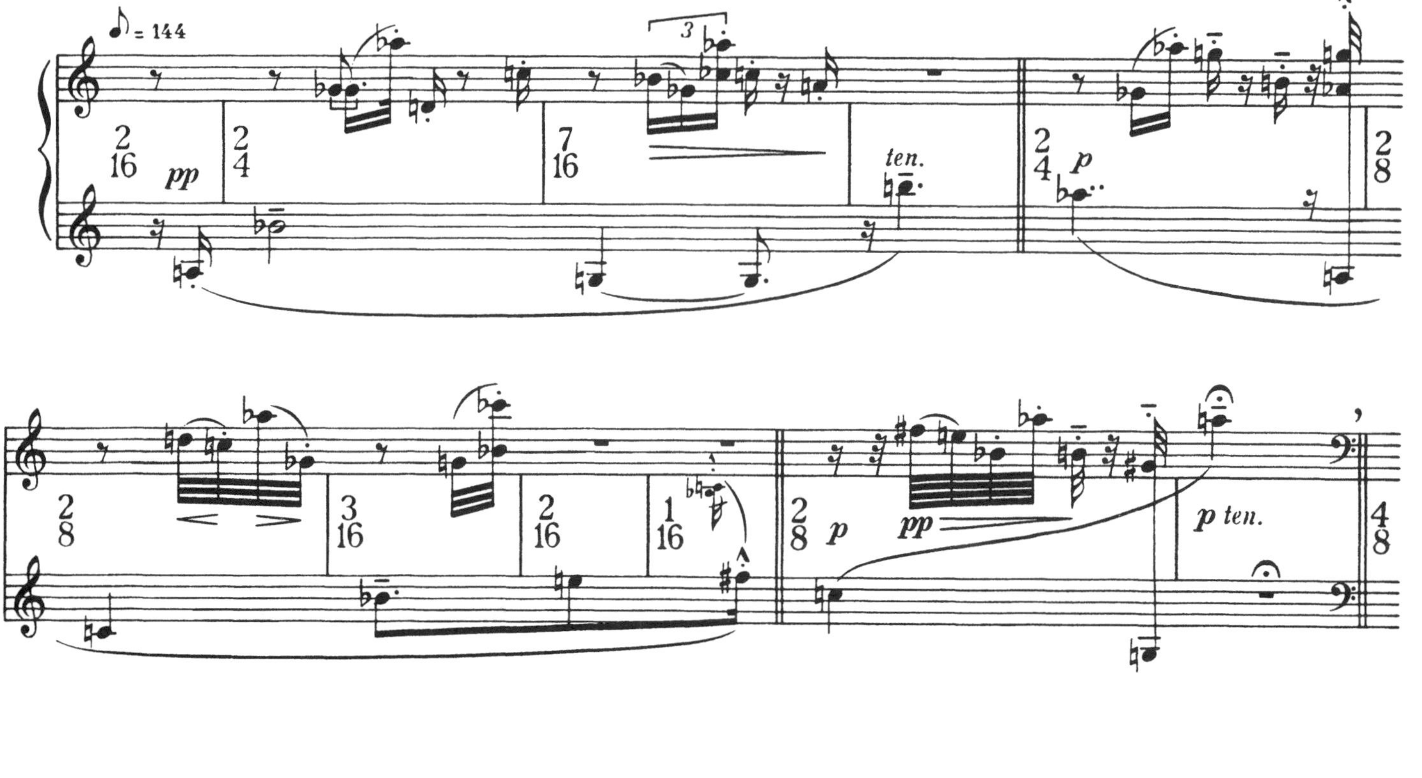

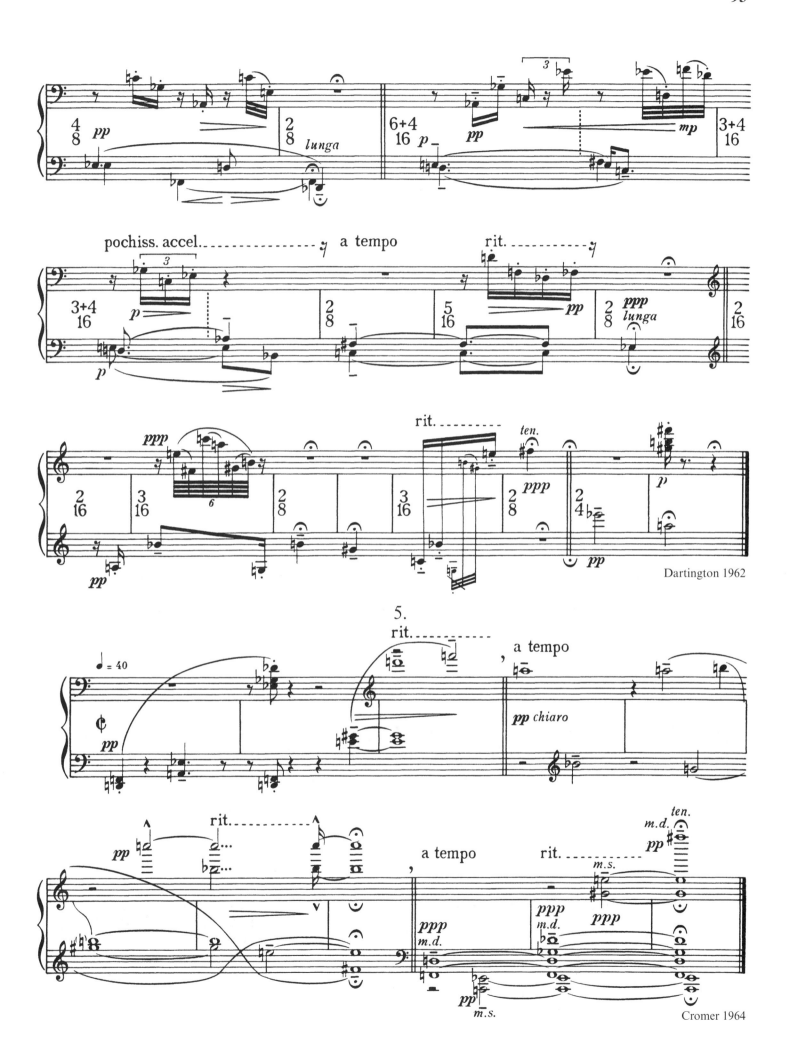

Dartington 1962

Cromer 1964

Three Sanday Places

for Dr. Thomas Daniel Schlee

1. Knowes o' Yarrow

PETER MAXWELL DAVIES
(2009)

2. Waters of Woo

to Colin for his fiftieth birthday

3. Kettletoft Pier

Yesnaby Ground
from *The Yellow Cake Revue*

PETER MAXWELL DAVIES
(1980)

This page intentionally left blank to facilitate page turns.

for Grace Cloutier

Aeolian Ballade

DAVID DEL TREDICI
(2007)

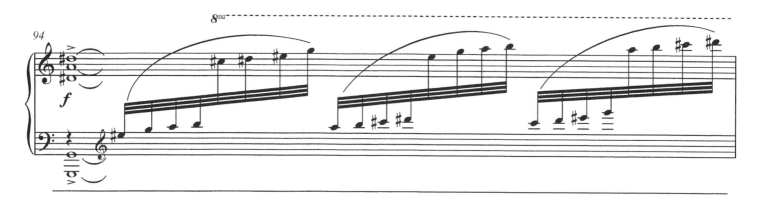

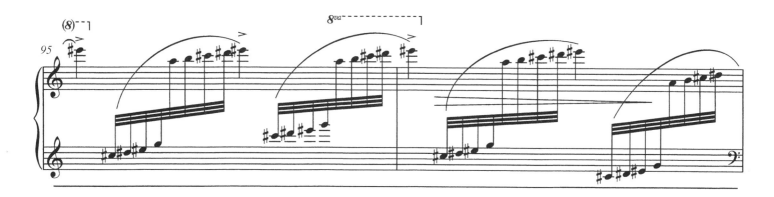

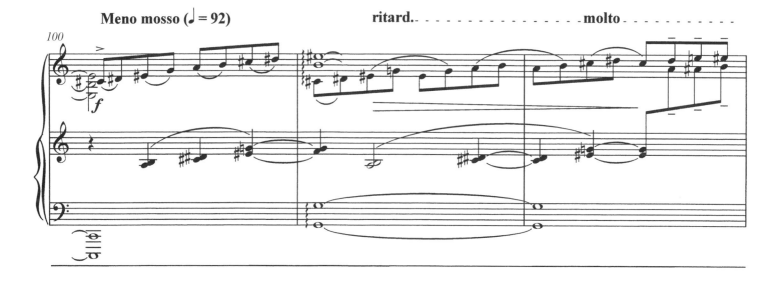

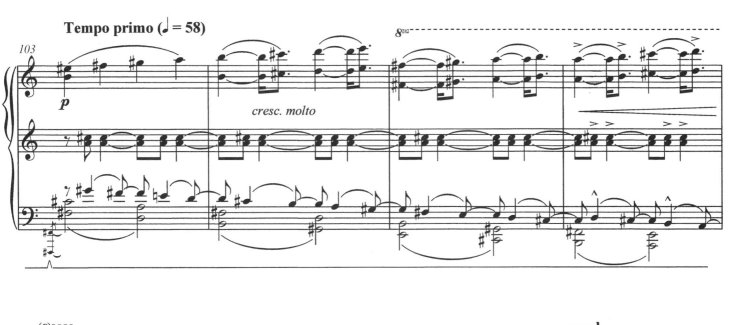

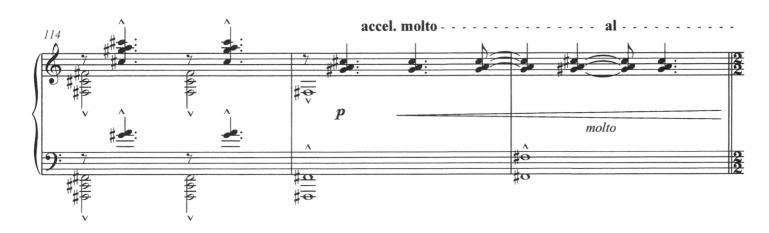

For Evlyn Howard-Jones

Five Piano Pieces
1. Mazurka

FREDERICK DELIUS
(1923)

For Yvonne O'Neill
2. Waltz

(1923)

For Evlyn Howard-Jones
3. Waltz

Croissy 1891
(finished at Grez sur Loing 1922)

4. Lullaby
for a modern baby

(1922)

(To be hummed or violin con sord.)

5. Toccata

To Catherine Murphy

Episodes
Vol. 1
1. First Lyric Piece

CARLISLE FLOYD
edited and fingered by the composer
(1965)

2. Second Lyric Piece

3. Scherzino

4. Third Lyric Piece

5. Fourth Lyric Piece

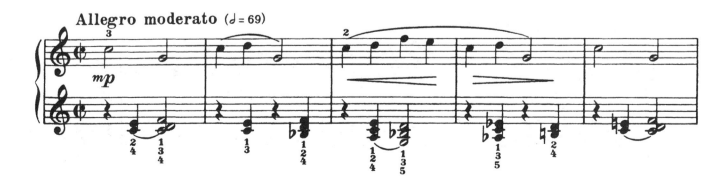

6. Marching Hymn

7. An Ancient Air

8. Arietta

9. Lullaby

10. Chorale

11. Ballad

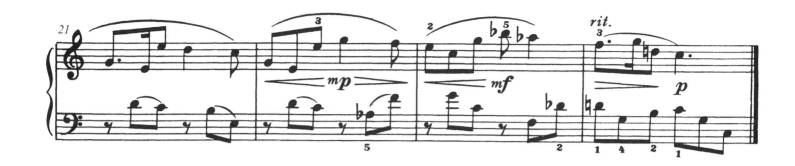

12. Pavane

13. Serenade

14. Wind Song

15. Burletta

Rhapsody

JOHN IRELAND
(1915)

for Llyr Williams

Madog

KARL JENKINS
(2009)

Moto perpetuo – in strict time ♩ = 236–240

Toccata

BENJAMIN LEES
(1947)

Railroad (Travel Song)

MEREDITH MONK
(1981)

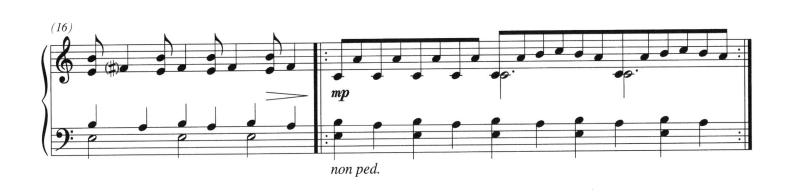

For Nurit Tilles

Window in 7's

MEREDITH MONK
(1986)

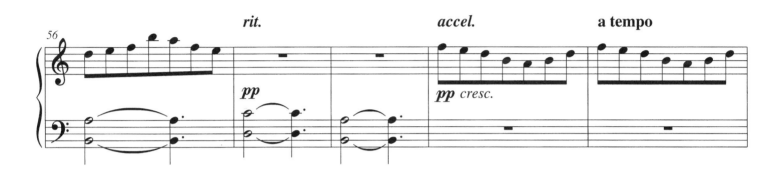

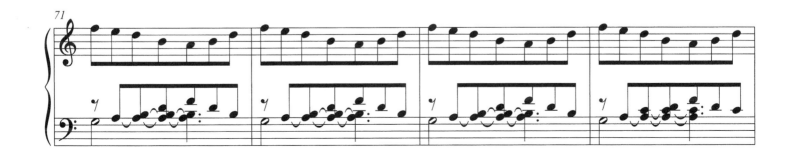

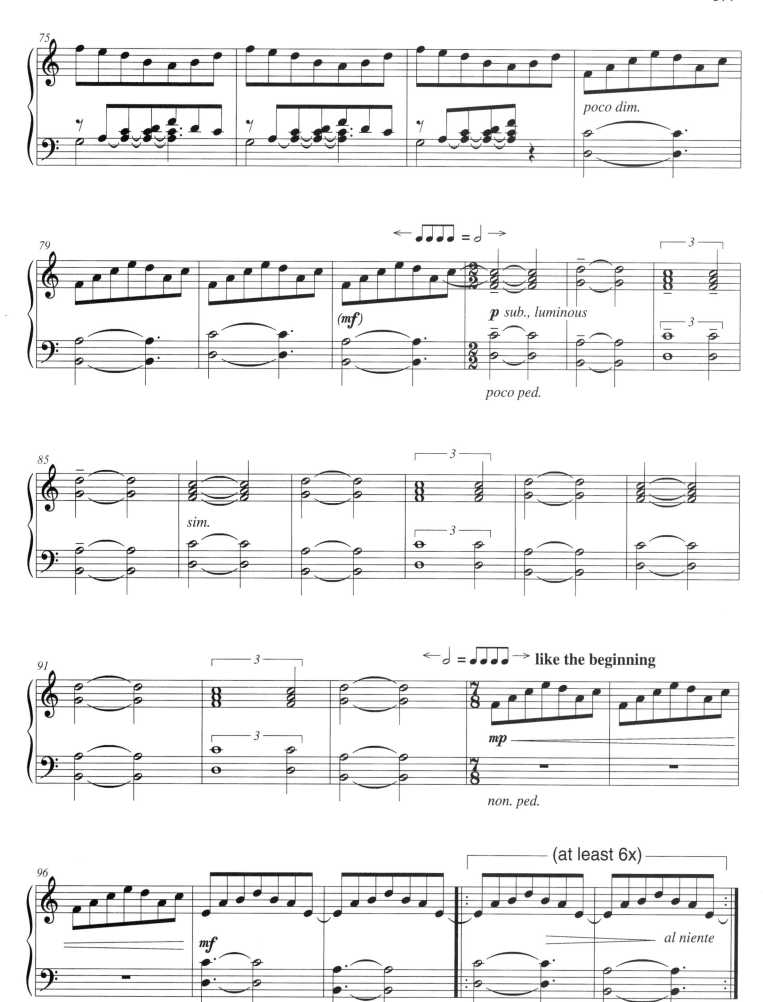

Six Friends

NED ROREM
(2006-07)

For Marian

8va **NY**
8 April 2006

For Barbara

NYC and Nantucket
Sept. 2006

For Rosemary

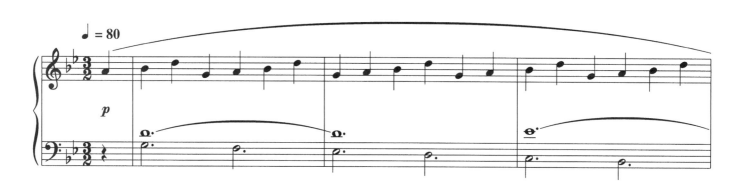

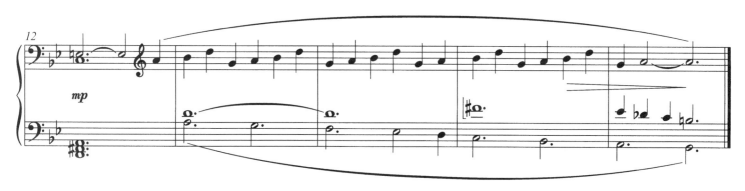

NYC
29 Dec. 2006

For Mary

29 Oct. 2006

For Don

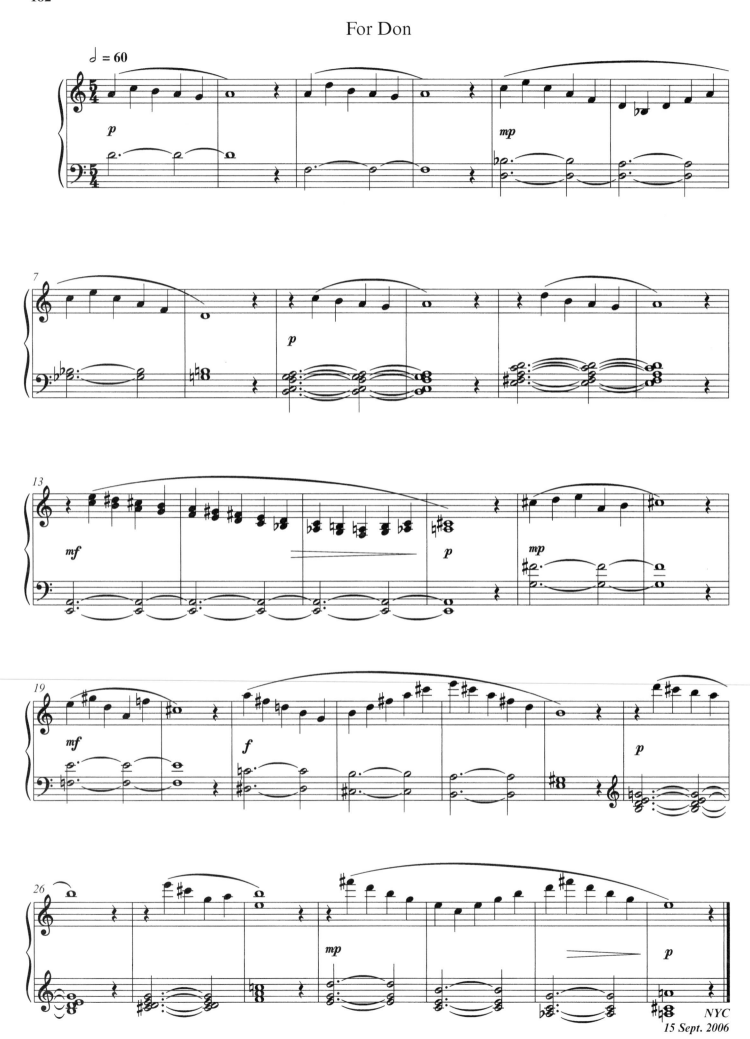

NYC
15 Sept. 2006

75 Notes for Jerry

January 2007

Franco Assetto: Drawing Virgil Thomson

VIRGIL THOMSON
(1981)

1' 00"
Corfu
August 23, 1981

Homage to Marya Freund and to the Harp

VIRGIL THOMSON
(1956)

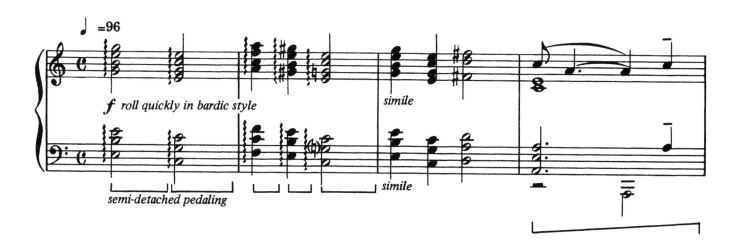

New York
July 25, 1956

Persistently Pastoral: Aaron Copland

VIRGIL THOMSON
(1942)

New York
October 16, 1942

This page intentionally left blank to facilitate page turns.

Old English Worthies

March

Wm. Richardson
ALEC ROWLEY
(1917)

Variations

Peter Lee of Putney
ALEC ROWLEY

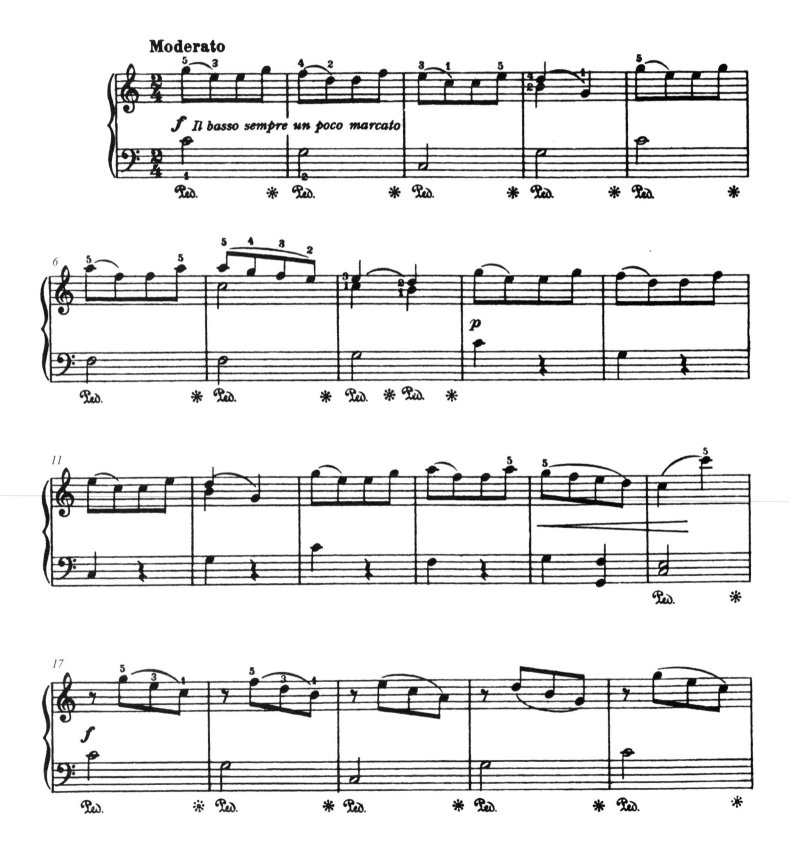

Menuet
(First published in 1711)

Jeremiah Clarke
ALEC ROWLEY

Hornpipe
The St. Catherine

John Barrett
ALEC ROWLEY

Christ-Church Bells

M. Camidge
ALEC ROWLEY

Saraband

Dr. J. Worgan
ALEC ROWLEY

The Prince's March

Anthony Young
ALEC ROWLEY

Invention

John Stanley
ALEC ROWLEY

Rigadoon
Rigaudon

William Babell
ALEC ROWLEY

Hunting Song

La chasse • La caza • Die Jagd

James Hook
ALEC ROWLEY